SEE BOB RUN
& WILD ABANDON
DANIEL MACIVOR

Playwrights Canada Press
Toronto

See Bob Run © 1987 *Wild Abandon* © 1988 Daniel MacIvor
Playwrights Canada Press
54 Wolseley St., 2nd fl. Toronto, Ontario CANADA M5T 1A5
Tel: (416) 703-0201 Fax: (416) 703-0059
e-mail: orders@puc.ca   http://www.puc.ca

Playwrights Canada Press acknowledges the support of The Canada
Council for the Arts for our publishing programme
and the Ontario Arts Council.

Cover photo: Keith Penner
Cover design: Tony Hamill

Canadian Cataloguing in Publication Data
MacIvor, Daniel, 1961
        See Bob run; &, Wild abandon
Plays

ISBN 0-88754-486-X

I. Title. II.: Wild Abandon
PS8575.186S4   1990   C812'.54   C90-09129-9
PR9199.3.M33S4   1990

First edition: March 1990. Second printing: August 1996.
Third printing: September 1999. Fourth printing: July 2001.
Printed and bound by Hignell Printing at Winnipeg, Manitoba, Canada.

CONTENTS

Author's Preface

See Bob Run is a play about love. And fear. *Wild Abandon* is a play about fear. And love. Beyond, within and around those statements I imagine there to be many other possibilities.

Probably because of the fact that I also performed it, I was often asked if *Wild Abandon* was autobiographical. It is no more autobiographical than is *See Bob Run*. No more and no less.

Performing and witnessing a one-person show is an experience like no other. The relationship between the audience and the "actor" is dangerously intimate, thrillingly immediate. I came to understand this when performing the second production of *Wild Abandon* because it lacked both those qualities. I allowed myself to become comfortable in "knowing" the piece, in knowing the questions before they were asked, and around that comfort is built an impenetrable wall which stands between actor and audience. A one-person show is not so much a performance as it is an admission. That admission must never be restricted.

And to each performer who may play a Bob or a Steve, see it as your autobiography. We are all somewhere in each of them.

Full of love and fear.

I would like to thank Albert Chevalier, Ken McDougall and Jerry Doiron for their support and belief in these plays.

Daniel MacIvor

SEE BOB RUN

For Caroline

See Bob Run was first produced by Buddies in Bad Times Theatre and Da Da Kamera at The Poor Alex Theatre, 1987, in Toronto.

BOB   *Caroline Gillis*

Directed by Ken McDougall.
Designed by Steve Mici Lucas.
Stage managed by Claudine Domingue.
Original music by Ron Doug Parks.

"Brought a Love" © Ron Doug Parks used by permission.

The Set

There should be no effort to create a "real" highway, a "real" car. It is as if Bob has rented the space and built the set to tell her story to this audience tonight.

In the Toronto production the set was a single bucket seat, a section of chain link fence stage left, a section of picket fence stage right. A dotted line ran up the centre isle of the theatre.

Act One

---

*The set: the trans-Canada highway. In the
middle of the road is a single car seat on a
platform. On one side a weather beaten
picket fence, on the other a rusted chain
link fence. The fences and highway bend
off into exaggerated perspective upstage.*

*Darkness. We hear "Brought a Love." It
fades. The sound of a car approaching.
Headlights move across the stage. In the
headlights we see a young woman sitting
in the car seat. Darkness. Another car.
Darkness. Another car. This time when
Bob is seen in the headlights they freeze
on her. They become bright. She steps out
of the seat.*

BOB   Once upon a time there was a King and a Queen. And
they were married. The King was handsome and strong
and everybody thought he was good cause he was, most
of the time, and he was good even to the Queen who was
a witch. She was ugly and mean and a witch who put
spells on people cause she hated everybody. That's how
she got the King to marry her, by putting a spell on him so
he'd think she was pretty and good and that. But she
wasn't. Aaaaaaand…all the King wanted was a Princess.
He wanted a Princess so bad. A Little Princess that he
could put on his knee and give big wet kisses to. And the

Queen says "No." "No way," she says. She don't want a
Princess cause she knows what'll happen. She knows that
the King will end up lovin the Princess so much that he
won't love her anymore—even though he hardly does
now anyway. That's when the King starts to get mad. He
wants a Princess. It's all he wants. And because she
won't give it to him he gets full of hate. Full of hate for
her. And they start fightin all the time. One night it gets
real bad and they both lose their voices from yellin about
the Princess. And then. The King grabs the Queen and
throws her down and makes her make sex right there on
the floor in the kitchen. The cold, cold kitchen floor.
They're doin it but they're not thinkin about love, they're
thinkin about hate. He's thinkin about how he's stabbin
her with his thing and she's thinkin about how she wishes
she could close herself up so tight she would cut it right
off him. And it's over. And they're layin there on the
floor in the kitchen starin at the ceilin and the King
reaches over and puts his hand on the Queen's belly and
he knows. He knows. She's pregnant. And she was it
turns out. That's what the doctor says. And the King is so
happy he's jumpin up and down and singin. The Queen
never seen him like that before. And she gets even worse.
More ugly, more stupid, more hateful. Cause she knows.
The King is gonna love the Princess more than her. So
she puts a spell on herself. She's a witch so she can do
that. And months and months go by and she's gettin
bigger and bigger. Lookin pregnant and that. Then, this
night, she starts gettin the pains that the baby's comin, so
the King runs and gets the Doctor. The Doctor comes and
goes in the Queen's room. The King's waitin outside the
door. He's waitin forever. Then, the part comes where
the baby's supposed to cry but the King don't hear nothin.
Another long time goes by and the King's freakin out that
somethin's wrong. Then he hears this sound. This long
loud ugly sound. And this gross smell. He doesn't know
what's goin on. Then finally out comes the Doctor and
he's got this look on his face and the King says "What?"

and the Doctor looks at the King and says...“The Queen wasn't pregnant at all; she was just full of shit.”

> BOB *laughs.*

The end.

> *It is night in a car.* BOB *speaks to the driver.*

Bob.
Roberta.
Bob.
East. I'm headed east. Until you hit water. Alot of water.

You don't got a radio in here?
Man that's pretty weird.
Only reason to have a car. Radio on wheels. Roll up the windows you got your own studio. Right? Drivin along bein in any band you want. Man, I'd have one. And speakers like this...huge. Make a wind. I always got a radio. I even got one in my bag but it needs electricity. I hate no music. You gotta have music man, it's the best. I like all kinds too. Every kind. Don't matter what as long as it's music. 'Cept for that stuff they play in offices and that so you don't even notice it. That's not music, that's just bad air. Pollution right. But every other kind I like. Even, like, Johnny Cash? You know. People think he's dumb but he's really not. He always wears black cause the world's so bad right. That's pretty neat. All kinds. You don't like it eh? Some people say it's just noise, but that's cause they're not really listenin. Once you listen to it, once you really listen to it...that's it, you're gone. Like me man. I'd die if I didn't have it eh. Makes me talk when I don't have music and I don't like talkin.

I don't usually talk this much...some people pick you up cause they need somebody to talk to drivin eh.
Them are the people who don't have radios.

Talkin talkin words words...all them words and nothin
gets said. That's why music's the best right. There's
words but then there's music to really make them mean
somethin. Like, you know what I mean?
Like, you can say: "Bob got a gun." Or, you can sing:
(*singing*) "Bob got a gun, oooo, Bob got a gun gun
gun...."
See. Singin makes it mean more.

BOB *laughs.*

Just kiddin buddy.
Just kiddin.

Black. Night in another car.

Bob.
Roberta.
Bob.

Nobody ever called me Roberta. Ever. Even when I was
just a baby. I think they only wrote "Roberta" on the
papers cause the doctors or priest or whoever wouldn't let
them put "Bob." No middle name either. Just Bob. My
mother wouldn't let them give me a middle name. "One
name's enough" she said. Easy to say and remember.
And spell. Just three little letters. Two the same. I think
it's okay though. Not like some dumb names. Like
Jennifer. What's a Jennifer? Or Linda. What's a Linda?
Even like, my best friend is Tamara, which sounds nice
but it's pretty dumb anyway right? Like, she herself says
it's dumb. Which it is. If you're gonna call somebody
somethin you should call them somethin that they're like.
I don't know if I'm like a Bob though. People say it's a
good name for me. Better than Roberta. This girl when I
was in school, Roberta Robina Bonaparte, she was fat and
had glasses. Her mother made her wear ugly clothes and
take tap dancin lessons...Man, I don't think dancin's

supposed to be noisy. Every time we had a show at
school Roberta'd do this bad tap dancin to that song
"Knock Three Times" by Tony Orlando and Dawn.
Which was a dumb song then even. She was a perfect
Roberta. You know?

If I had a kid, and I doubt it, but if I did I'd name it Shiny.
Shiny.
Cause that's what I'd want it to be.
You know what I mean?

Do radio's cost extra in cars or what?

> *Black. Gentle light up slowly. A car.* BOB
> *is sleeping.*

Timmy...

> *The car stops suddenly and* BOB *is jerked
> awake.*

Jesus! What...? Oh shit man... No that's okay that's okay.
Shit. I was sleepin... I was...I was havin a dream
about... Where are we?
Timmy? What about Timmy? Yeah? What I say?
Just "Timmy?"
That's my ex-boyfriend. What I say? Nothin—just
"Timmy?"
Why was I sayin that I wonder.
I wasn't dreamin about him. I was dreamin about...this
great dream...standin in the water right up to my
neck...and there's that big weird animal...Timmy wasn't
there though. He wasn't anywhere. He's my
ex-boyfriend. But I don't know if he knows he's my
ex-boyfriend or not. I suppose he does eh. Cause I'm
here and he's there. Too bad some ways. We had a band
right? "Finger Prince." It was his band really. He was
Timmy Prince. It was his band but he let me join up. And

not just cause I was his girlfriend either. It was cause I
sing great back-up and I'm a wicked dancer. That's what
he said. It was so good at first. Before he got fucked.
Excuse my language.
You never heard a song until you heard Timmy Prince
sing it. That's what everybody used to say. He could
clean the air with his singin. Like it wasn't a pretty voice
but it was really real. Right from his heart. People would
shut right up and listen. Even drunk. It was somethin.
Best band I ever heard cause of Timmy. Tamara said he
was gonna be a star eh? A big one. He thought I was
good too. At the end before the band split up he even had
me singin lead on a song. "Baby Tonight." Dylan right?
I'd sing lead he'd sing back-up. It was excellent. We put
it right at the end of the last set. There'd be people cryin.

Too bad what happened but it had to.
I don't wanna talk about that.

You ever play that game?
When you were a kid?
"Who Falls Dead The Best?" We played it up in the
graveyard. One person starts as gunner and everybody
else took turns runnin by and gettin shot and whoever
falls dead the best gets to be gunner.
We played it on this big triangle of grass...in the
graveyard. There'd be like fifteen of us playin.
Everybody doin all this fancy dyin, flyin through the air
or rollin down the hill or doin spins. Most people died
like it was a kinda dance. We played all the time. It was
our game.

Weird eh?

It's not really like that you know.

> *Black. Lights up.* BOB *is standing at the
> side of the road waiting for a ride.*

No cars. She waits. She begins to sing
softly to herself and slowly realizes she is
alone and liking the sound of her voice on
the empty highway. She increases her
volume. She gets very loud. A dog begins
to bark. Another. Every dog within five
miles.

Shit.

Black. BOB *in a spot.*

There was this big weird animal in the closet. This big
weird animal. And it was in the closet. The little girl who
was born a Princess and a pile of shit is always scared
when she goes to bed at night cause she knows it's there.
She can see it peakin out and she can hear it breathin.
Breathin. It's real for sure. But no one else believes her
and call her dreamin when she talks about it. A bad
dream. And she says, "But there is an animal in the
closet, I can hear it breathin!" And the mother says "Shut
up. Grow up. Bad dream." And after a while she starts
thinkin maybe it is a dream. And just when she starts
believin that, that's the night the door of the closet opens
and there it is. This big weird naked animal. And it's
smilin. But not friendly. Or too friendly so it's scary.
And it comes over to her in her bed where she's starin at it
and it says: "Hold on to my handle, do that. See it, there's
my happy handle. Come on. Hold on to it and make me
happy." So she does cause she doesn't want to make it
mad. So she does and she makes it happy. And the big
weird animal is so happy it never goes back into the closet
again. It's always waitin for her. But it's okay for the
little girl now. Now she knows, it's just a dream.

Black. Night in another car.

Bob.
Just Bob.
Cause it's just Bob that's all.

You got a cigarette?
Too bad.
Yeah cancer. Bad stuff.

Cancer's really weird eh? Like you can look smooth and
clean on the outside but inside you're all rotten and
black... Like bad people. Like my mother. She's really
ugly and mean inside but if you were standin behind her
in line at the grocery store she'd let you get in front of her
if you had less stuff or if you came to the door sellin a
chocolate bar for kids with no legs she'd buy one or even
maybe two...she tricks everybody. Makes them think
she's good. But she's not. My father told me how she
really was. See, she even had me tricked for awhile cause
I remember once I got this flu and she comes into the
living room where I'm sleepin and she sits by me and puts
my head on her lap, my face is pressin right up against her
good skirt makin it all wet with my sweat but she don't
care and she was doin this to my hair...See, she was
trickin me. She can't be good cause...she can't be good
cause she kicked my father out for nothin. I come home
one day from school and Children's Aid is there and she's
pretendin to be cryin and she says to me, in front of them
right, she says, "It's okay baby, he's gone, he won't come
back and he won't be able to hurt you anymore." He
never hurt me...never...just loved me more that's
all...just loved me more...

Pause.

She's livin with this guy now who smells so bad.

Pause.

You ever kill anybody?

> *Black.* BOB *is standing left of the car*
> *seat. The seat is not visible.*

Tamara and me would get all dressed up to go out. She
had the greatest stuff. Leopard skin jumpsuit she always
let me wear. And she had these wicked, wicked boots.
Fringes on em. She'd be walkin in em and it'd be like
there were waves movin around her ankles. So we'd get
all dressed up. Lookin really hot with the perfect earrings.
And then we'd take a taxi down the Corral. Get there
about ten, ten thirty, dependin on the band, and walk in at
the break. The guys would look at us and be droolin and
the girls would look at us like sluts or lovin Tamara's
boots or whatever. At the bar we'd each order a Zombie
and two beers. By the time the band started playin again
we'd be ready to have a good time. Yeah! Dancin! So
wild. The band would be lovin us cause we were part of it
and makin everybody dance. After a while they'd start
playin everything right to us, especially the slow ones.
Like "Angie" and Spyder's song about "Love Me Now"
or whatever. I'd get off so bad. It was perfect cause I was
imaginin that it was me they were singin about or that I
was in the band doin backup. Tamara though, she liked it
cause she could see which guy she wanted or which guy
wanted her. She had a way to do it. First the lead singer,
then the bass player, then the other guys, and always the
drummer last. She said to save the best for last. Mostly
all I wanted was to be in the band...Tamara wanted the
band to be in her. Yeah, yeah that's it eh. I wanted to be
in the band and Tamara wanted the band to be in her.

Then there's that night I will never forget. Everything
goes the same except we're goin to see Finger Prince
which I never seen but Tamara did one time at Backstreet.
She says, "You gotta see em Bob." So I figure she thinks
she can get one of em. But she was right man. I had to

see em. I had to see Timmy Prince. Man he was
somethin. He was the world. And it was when he was
singin, even his own songs, that he was the most beautiful
thing I ever before saw. He was more than a person. I'm
so flipped out I never even had a sip of the Zombie.
Freakin. Like, I gotta meet him after the last set. Tamara
gets us back to the change room. I'm standin there in
front of him not sayin nothin like I was retarded or
somethin. After awhile he looks up at me and smiles and
says "Hello Princess."

Black. Night in another car.

Nice car for a girl.
You make alot of money?
I wish.
Maybe I'll get somethin where I'm goin.
East.
To the water.

Pause.

Jeeze...Bob.
Yeah! Roberta yeah!
That's pretty neat, nobody ever gets that.
Yeah I think it's good too.
Just Bob though.
Nobody ever calls me Roberta.
No. I usta have a boyfriend but not anymore. Not since
three o'clock. And I'm not gonna have another one for a
long time either. Maybe never. No way. It's too dumb
and fake. And it gives me a headache. You know? Yeah,
girls are better. You should meet my best friend Tamara.
Man she's got it right. She don't let no guy take her
noplace she don't wanna go. She's got balls this big. I
shoulda told her I was leavin but I didn't have time, you
know. I'll write her a letter though once I get where I'm
goin. Maybe she'll come down or somethin.

What?
What? What do ya mean?
I don't...Hey, I don't like that okay.
I don't do that okay.

I'll get out right up here.

I'm not scared.

This is far enough.
Stop. Stop the fuckin car lady!

> BOB *gets out of the car.*

Jesus.
Nobody's safe from nobody no more or fuckin what!

> BOB *crosses the stage.*

I told my mother to get fucked and I left.
I even said that to her.
"GET FUCKED WOMAN!"
And I left and I went to stay at Tamara's place.
Sometimes I stayed in Tamara's bed with her cause it was
a big bed and there was nothin wrong with that. And
sometimes I would let her hold me cause she was lonely
and she'd be cryin. Everybody gets lonely. Like I even
wore her clothes. It was like we were sisters. I would
like it when she held me. She was so soft. It wasn't sick
though. If I was sad it would make me feel better too. It
wasn't sick. It was just two sisters who were sad.
And that's where I was stayin when I met Timmy.
Tamara hated Timmy.
Maybe she was jealous but there's nothin wrong with that.
We were the best friends in the world.
She'd be happy now though I bet eh.
Timmy said she was a weirdo. She isn't a weirdo. Well.
Maybe she is but if she is it's in a good way. The first

night I met her she was so great. Like I'm at a party at
Leo's place and I was drinkin hard liquor and smokin
somethin. Stupid. Cause now I know I can't do that
without freakin out. Man that night I was so flipped. I'm
sittin on the steps at Leo's and I think I'm dyin. And then
Tamara who I never even met before comes out and sits
on the steps way over on the other side. Starin at me outta
the corner of her eyes. Then she says to me, really
serious: "You're not gonna stab me or anything are you?"
And I say "No." And she says, "Good, cause everybody
in there is." And we're real quiet. Then she starts laughin,
at herself. Then I start laughin cause she was freaked out
the same way I was, and just because she laughed so
funny. She laughs like this like hardly any sound comes
out but her whole body's shakin and her face is froze up
like this...
She laughs so funny.
Then, all of a sudden she jumps off the steps and starts
dancin. Like there's no music but she grabs me and gets
me to dance too. Then she says, "Come on!" and we go
dancin up the middle of the street to the Donut Castle.
We get inside and some dumb station is on the radio, like
Englebert Humperdink, but we're still dancin.
Everybody's lookin at us like we're nuts. And I like that
you know? Sort of like we knew somethin they didn't.
We had this secret.

We order like six Apple Crullers and six Bavarian
Creams. Sat in the window and laughed and pigged out
for about an hour. And that's even before I knew her
name.

Then we're best friends. She says I can stay at her place
to get away from my mother. And she gets me a job at the
Beauty Parlour cause I didn't have one and I think we
spent every single minute together. Every single minute
for four months up until the second night of Finger Prince.

The second night of Finger Prince I went back to the
Corral by myself. I sat right at the front of the stage cause
I wanted to make sure Timmy Prince seen that I was
there. He seemed so big and like he wasn't a person. He
was like a song and from where he was standin he could
reach down and pick me up in his hands. He could hold
me way up above the ground where nobody could get me
and there'd be this music...

After the last song he comes over to me and wants to
drive me home. I say no I like walkin.
He leaves his car at the Corral and walks me.
We walk through the park and he tells me how the moon
is really no light at all, just gets it from the sun. And how
lilacs are the best flowers cause nobody ever has to plant
them and they just grow every year. All by themselves.
Cause they want to. And that I should have a lake named
after me. Lake Bob. And how he wishes he could bring
me one.
All this perfect pretend.
And that's what was good see.
For awhile.
Everything was like walkin through the park and
pretendin. He never tried nothin. I never thought of it.
I just wondered why he was wantin to talk to me all the
time.
Tamara nearly had a fit this one time he comes to work to
see me. Had a fit. She said cause we were busy. I say
cause he brought me lilacs and a card with the moon on it.
And nothin happened for a long time.
And then. That night on Tamara's sofa.
So quiet. Shh!
I don't remember it. I don't remember any of it.
Just after and how he looked like he was just a
person...real...Like it wasn't Timmy Prince holdin me so
quiet and dressin slow and leavin backwards out Tamara's
front door. Just some person...some guy. Like the ones
in school and the ones on the street.

After and me thinkin of how I was feelin this way I never
felt before and the start of gettin sick.

After he goes home I took this bath so hot that next day it
was like I had a sunburn.

And he wants me to move in and I say no.

And he wants me to move in and I say no.

And he wants me to move in and he brings me this bottle
of pink water.

I say "What is it?" He says: "It's your Lake Bob."

And I say yes I'll move in. Cause that wasn't real—see it
was pretend and maybe he would be able to pretend
forever.

But no.

And he's so gentle and soft, and every time it happens the
sick gets worse. Cause it's all a lie see. That part's just for
him.

It's supposed to hurt. But he kept wantin me to feel good
in it.

That's not how it's supposed to be. All that gentle. It's a
lie. When it's real it's a lie.

Only pretend is true.

I know that. Now I know.

It's all about...I know see...It's all about when I was
little...a little kid. I know that now. I'm asleep. Or
almost asleep. And he comes into my room. But I don't
open my eyes. And he's scared you can tell. He is. He
sits down at the edge of the bed. For this long time. And
after awhile

he...pulls...down...the...blanket...and...lifts...up...my...
shirt...and...rubs...his...hand...on...my...belly...and...
says...

Shhh.

Shhh. I'm not supposed to tell anybody. Cause Mommy's
so mean to him.

And that it might hurt. And it does hurt...but that isn't the
important part. Don't think about the hurt...

Shhh.

Think about the water. All this water over you and the

sound of waves. The important part is that I am his
Princess.
And I am his Princess...and he loves me more
than...more than...more than anything anyone even the
smartest man in the world can think off...and...Daddy!
Shhh.
We'll just cuddle. Shhh we'll cuddle. I'll hold you and
hold you my little Princess. Shhh Princess. Beautiful,
beautiful, shhh...
And I will never go away and I will always always no
matter what be your Daddy.
And he went away and never said nothin not even
goodbye. And I know he's at the water.
Isn't he?

Black. BOB *is leaning into a car..*

You married?
I said are you married?
Good.

BOB *gets in.*

This your husband's car?
Oh yeah? Must be nice.
East.
Uh...Jennifer..
I'm goin east to meet my father.

Your husband give you this car?
It's nice.
I don't even know how to drive.

You love him eh?
Your husband.
Good. That's good. It's good you love somebody.
Nobody can stop you.

I'm just gonna go to sleep now okay.
That okay?

You ever been to the water?
It's nice eh?
I bet it is.
I can't wait to be there.
I'm just gonna walk in up to my neck first thing.

Right up to my neck and just stand there.

Imagine what that'd be like eh?

> *Lights fade. Bright headlight from the first scene.*

So there's this dance. This big huge dance where you
have to go with someone and wear flowers. Everybody's
supposed to ask someone special to go with them. All the
people from all around are going. They're going to have
this special kind of romantic music and millions of
kleenex decorations. The little girl who is a Princess and
a pile of shit is going. She asks the big weird animal to
go with her. Not cause she's scared but cause she wants
him to. See it's just that he's weird not that he's mean.
And he loves her so so much. Really really. More than
anything. The big weird animal says yes and he's so
happy because he would love to go to the dance with the
little girl. And it's exciting cause it's so special. They go.
They get there. They walk in. Everybody stops.
Everybody stops talkin and dancin and havin fun. All the
nice romantic music stops. They are starin at the big
weird animal and the little girl. Some of the people start
pointin and laughin, some of them leave and some of
them are so scared they get angry and say "Who let that
thing in here?!". And it's just cause they're stupid or
cause they don't understand that it's the most beautiful
and perfect thing...the big weird animal and the little girl.

Nobody understands…And there's this witch there and
she…No. The witch isn't there. But everybody's standin
around laughin and yellin and that makes the big weird
animal start to cry cause he's not mean at all and he's got
the biggest, softest heart. So the little girl says, "Don't
cry okay, don't cry, you're not bad, don't cry." And she
takes him by the hand and she starts dancin with him in
the middle of all these people, all around them, real quiet.
They're dancin so slow and romantic and exquisite. The
music starts again and it's perfect and the big weird
animal stops cryin and starts smilin and they're the most
excellent dancers. The most excellent dancers and other
people start dancin again and other people until
everybody's dancin again and everybody understands now
and it's okay cause it's so good and all the people have the
best time of their lives and the big weird animal and the
little girl get the award for best dancers and the dance
goes on and on and on…

That whole last part isn't true.

> *The light shifts suddenly.* BOB *steps
> downstage.*

I bet you could go downtown I bet in the middle of the
day and stand on the corner and start screamin your head
off—just screamin and makin noise and not stop—and
they'd call some cops that'd take you away to some
hospital where they'd stick a needle in your arm and then
put you on some freak floor poppin a different colour pill
in your mouth every ten minutes and I bet nobody'd even
ask you "What's wrong?".

> BOB *opens her mouth to scream. A siren.
> Black. Lights up in the car.*

Shit man what's that? What they want? What's goin on?
What were you doin? Were you speedin or somethin?

Why were you doin that, what were you doin?
Jesus, I hate cops man. Well pull over or somethin!

The siren passes.

Oh. Man. It looked like they were after us though eh?
Didn't it?
Shit I was freakin.
Probably on their way to arrest some old lady for jay
walkin. Man they give me the creeps so bad. Like they
can just walk up to you and arrest you or hit you or
somethin just cause they don't like the way you look.
That's scary eh? It's not even the guns though. It's the
sticks. Those sticks. Oh man. The guns don't bug me.
Daddy always had guns. Even taught me how to use em.
They're not scary at all, cept if they don't work when you
want em to. But the sticks. I never had any trouble with
the cops. Timmy though. Shit. He was always gettin
arrested for somethin. Just cause what he looked like.
Cause he wasn't bad or anything you know. He wasn't
mean really. It was a different kind of mean...Know what
I'm talkin about? You know what I'm talkin about?
That's what drives me crazy that nobody does.

BOB *stands and steps forward.*

Nobody knows what I'm talkin about.
Tamara said she did sort of.
I don't know if really.
See, when he was singin he was, he was...not real. And
when he was talkin about lilacs and lakes and moons he
was...not real. Sometimes it was so pretend it was
perfect. Then he writes me this song. I didn't want him
to, I said don't sing it but he did. It made me out to be
something...special...and I'm not...see...I'm not
special...at all. This song was "Brought A
Love"...(*singing*) "I brought a love, in a cage, to your
house, darling, and I let it go..." Him lookin at me and

singin...It would make me feel real sick...throw up kinda
sick. And he'd get me on the bed. His mouth over my
mouth and my eyes and my face and I couldn't breathe
and he was suffocatin me, it was like, and I'd be starin at
a picture or the ceiling, it's all hot and wet and he presses
into me so I can't move and he's sayin "I love you I love
you I love you" in this low voice all heavy and "it feels so
good, don't it feel good"...and NO it don't...this the bad
part...this is the part where you're supposed to
pretend...and these feelings...and I'm scared I'm gonna
get sick all over the place...one time I almost was...but I
got up and run out the back door and over the fence and
all the way past the store. To I don't even know where
just runnin. Legs goin so far apart it's like I'm gonna split
in two. And I only stopped cause my head hurt and I fell
down. Maybe I never would of stopped. Maybe I would
of run right to the water. That's where I was goin I bet. I
never been there you know...when I was a Princess...and
in my room...and it was so dark...Daddy usta
say...Shhh... "Think about the water"...the water knows
everything...it knows everybody's biggest secrets...and it
turns them into the sound of the waves at night and then
it's okay cause everybody loves the sound of the waves at
night. The water whisperin everybody's biggest secrets to
you and you dream them nice. No bad dreams no scary
dreams only nice dreams from it. And he promised me
that someday...

Someday Princess I'll take you to the water and you'll see
and you'll hear...
And...I gave him my special and he took it with him
when he went. That's where he went to. To the water.
I bet.

Black. Another car.

It's gettin cold eh? Brr. My hands are froze off.
Good thing you're a priest. There's alot of weirdos out
there. Priests are pretty safe eh?

My mother's livin in sin with this guy.

She kicked my father out for nothin.
Cause she didn't want me to have shit.
Cause I was shit. Excuse my language.

That's where I'm goin now.
To meet my father at the water.

I haven't been to confession since I was ten.
My mother didn't even care if I went to church.
I only usta go with my father. Daddy'd help me get
dressed up and we'd go Sunday morning and sit right up
in the front row and he'd hold my hand.

I still remember most of the stuff.
I do. Bless me father...Bless me father...for I have
sinned...it's been...a million years since my last
confession and these are my sins...
See.

Do you think God cares? If you do something that you
have to? Like if some people think it's a sin but it isn't? I
mean if you gotta do it?

Like nothin.

Do soldiers go to hell?
For killin people I mean?
That's weird.

He wasn't bad to me you know. Not bad. It was just
that...he stopped pretendin. But he was never bad to me

and he never hit me, well only one time but I hit him first.
Sometimes I wanted him to be bad. Smash me up against
the refrigerator so I'd get knocked out. Or get killed. So I
could get out. Cause he was doin it on purpose. Sayin he
loved me and that just to make me do it. He made me.
Keepin at me all the time. "C'mere Baby, c'mere
Princess." I wasn't his Princess. He made me you know?
Fuck him eh? Just fuck him. FUCK YOU TIMMY
PRINCE. FUCK YOU YOU SON OF A BITCH!

> *The car stops suddenly.* BOB *is thrown*
> *from her seat into the darkness. The car*
> *light fades. A new light.* BOB *is sitting on*
> *the floor.*

And so. And so. And so. I come home from work and I
hate it. Shampooin hair in some stupid beauty parlour
with all these stupid people and these weirdo guys who
give me the creeps. And Tamara isn't talkin to me for
some stupid thing I didn't even do. Forgettin her birthday
or somethin. How can I FORGET it when I don't even
know when it is. "Well when is it then? When was it, I
never knew when it was, nobody told me." But she won't
say nothin and just keeps on not talkin to me. And I come
home. And there he is. There he is. Sittin on a kitchen
chair in the livingroom. I hate that so much. Kitchen
chairs are for the kitchen. And the TV is on some stupid
kind of movie they put on in the afternoon for people who
are scared to go outside. And he starts. "C'mere."
"C'mere." But ugly. Ugly like he knows I'm not comin
here. I'm goin to have a beer cause I'm hot but there's
none. So I go into the bedroom cause I'm gonna listen to
some music or somethin but he comes in. He's sayin all
this junk but I'm not sayin nothin back cause I don't
wanna. And he knocks all my stuff on the floor off the
dresser. Like that's gonna make me say somethin but it
don't. I got nothin to say just "leave me alone" but I'm
sick of sayin that. LEAVE ME ALONE. And he goes

outa the room. It's quiet. Shh. Quiet. Good. That's
good. Quiet. All of a sudden. First real low. He's playin
the guitar. So low I'm not sure if I'm really hearin it or if
it's just in my head but then he starts singin. Singin..."I
brought a love, in a cage, to your house, darling, and I let
it go..." Singin that, which I don't want to hear which I
really really don't want to hear. Starts singin it louder. I
slam the door. More loud then. Loud like I never thought
he could sing that loud. Could anyone ever sing that
loud? "I brought a love in a cage to your house darling
and I let it go..." I got my hands over my ears but I can
still hear it. I can still hear it like I'm listenin. But I don't
wanna. God! Shit! STOP! STOP! And I get up off the
floor cause I'm on the floor. I get up off the floor and I go
over to the closet. I start pullin stuff out. Diggin through
all this stuff. Lookin for it. Lookin. I know it's there.
And there it is. The box with the big thick mailman's
elastics around it cause the top is broke. I open it up and
I'm thinkin about how it was a present from Daddy but he
never really gave it to me but it was the one he taught me
on and he never took it with him when he left like he
wanted me to have it. And there's already bullets in it
from long, long ages ago. All I'm thinkin is what if it
don't work. What if it don't work? That's in my head but
not in my body. My body gets up and walks the long way
around through the kitchen to the living room. Not even
scared. But my head's freakin out. What if it don't work?
What if it don't work? And he's still singin. Loud loud
loud and fast. I think I'm cryin. Or my head is. I'm
standin right in front of him now. I got it pointed at him.
Right at his head. And he knows I'm there and he won't
open his eyes and he won't stop singin and he won't stop
singin that song...and what if it don't work...and stop.
Stop. Stop! Stop! STOP! STOP...
And it worked.
Bang.

Black. Another car. The radio is playing.

Okay if I turn off the radio.
I got this kind of headache.

Thanks.

Alota noise in my head.
And can't keep a ride.
Nobody's ever goin farther than a mile east.
Rides and rides and rides.
Shit. It's hard you know. If you ever do it it's hard.

> BOB *removes her sweater revealing a*
> *blood stained t-shirt.*

Look.
My t-shirt's got all that blood in it.
I can't get it out.
I tried to but it won't come.

And you pick him up and...

> BOB *holds her hands as if cradling a*
> *head in her lap.*

I was really little and so sick...my mother's goin out
somewheres...she comes and sits by me and puts my head
in her lap, my face is pressin right up against her good
skirt makin it all wet with my sweat but she don't even
care...and she was doin this to my hair...like this...

Made this neat little hole in the middle of his forehead.
Neat little hole. Then...
Then I see the mess. And in it there's these pieces.
Where the back of his head come off. Three little
triangles.
Three of em.
I wanna pick them up and see if they fit together.

Like a jigsaw puzzle.
You think they would?

Are we stoppin?

Hey! You see that?
That was lilacs.
Right on the side of the highway like that. Nothin else
around.
They just grow by themselves you know. Nobody's gotta
plant em or anything.
Grow just cause they want to.
I think...you know...it's good we're stoppin...I think
maybe we should go someplace and I should tell
somebody about Timmy. Cause he's there all by
himself...it's so messy...You think? I better eh?

I mean it wasn't like he was so bad or anything.

> *As the car light fades* BOB *walks*
> *downstage into new light.* BOB *is holding*
> *the pink dress.*

Someday. Someday the little girl grows up. And she is
not a Princess and she is not a pile of shit. And she buys
some of that wallpaper. That wall paper you see places.
And in the catalogue. Where it's a picture? A picture of
the woods or a picture of the mountains or a picture of a
beach. She gets that wallpaper. The picture of a beach
and fills up the whole wall in her bedroom with it. And
puts tons of sand all over the floor. This deep with sand.
So the room is like a beach. And that's where she sleeps.
No walls no doors no windows. Just beach. And that's
where she wakes up. And she would love to one day
wake up and walk out in to the water right up to her neck.

Imagine what that'd be like eh?

We hear BOB and TIMMY *singing
Dylan's "Baby Tonight." BOB listens and
sways to the music.*

The End.

WILD ABANDON
The Study of Steve

For V.S.

Wild Abandon was first produced by Sword Theatre in association with Theatre Passe Muraille, 1988, in Toronto.

STEVE   Daniel MacIvor

Directed by Vinetta Strombergs.
Designed by Stephan Droege.
Slides by Steve Mici Lucas.
Stage managed by Chris Humphrey.
Original music by Zang Tumb Tumb.

The Set

For the Toronto production the set was a "black box." The props were a wooden chair, a chain, a white birdcage and an oversized egg. The back wall was a scrim on which the words and images were projected. While other options are possible, STEVE is a low-tech character most comfortable in low-tech surroundings.

The Images

Slides should be kept to a minimum. Photographic images should be black and white and text should be white typewritten words on a black background. Unless otherwise noted, slide images come up, wait a beat, then black out.

Act One

A chair sits centrestage. Lights up on
STEVE *standing behind the scrim.*

STEVE   (*voice over*) "Come into my parlour" said the poet to the
chair.
"Can't you see that I'm so lonely and I have no one to
care? My clothes are torn and smelling of an unrequited
love."
The poet slumped, he rubbed his eyes, he asked the one
above:
"Tell that chair to come in here and keep me from myself!
My soul has been alone too long upon that dusty shelf."

The chair sat in silence.
The poet was inspired.

Black. Lights up on STEVE *stage left.*

One time? I was a little kid like nine—this woman?
We were out in some stupid family rest-o-rant and
everybody's fighting in low voices and complaining about
the food and that, and this woman, sitting over across at
another table, she keeps looking at me, staring at me. I
don't say nothing and I start thinking: she's really staring
okay! and I start thinking: "Hey! This woman, she's my
real mother right. She followed me here. She's been
watching me for weeks and she's my real mother and
she's gonna come over and say 'This boy is my son' and
take me away from my stupid ugly family who won't let

me do nothing and never let me talk and never let me
listen and won't let me have a black room. She'd take me
away and out into her new car—that smells new and—a
convertible and—with the roof down and we'd drive far
away to this house—this castle she lives in and I'd live
there too and I'd have my own huge fucking room...
So I'm thinking this and the woman, she gets up and starts
walking over to me. I'm thinking: "HOLY SHIT! HOLY
SHIT! It really IS my mother!" I got so nervous. She
comes right up to me. Standing right there. I'm sitting
down okay, she's right there, and she reaches back...and
jabs this fork into my stomach and starts screaming:
DEVIL'S EYES DEVIL'S EYES DEVIL'S EYES!

        Pause.

The place went nuts. They had to take me to the
hospital...took her away to some rubber room
someplace...
Yeah.

That was pretty much the highlight of my life. That and
the time Alphonse McKeigan killed the duck in
Wentworth Park.

        Black. SOUND *is of people learning*
        dance steps. IMAGE *is of "Dancing."*
        Light on STEVE, *down centre, wrapped*
        in chains.

There are all kinds of different kinds of dancing.
Oh yeah. Tons. Well, four. Yeah. Four.
One. Stage dancing. The kind they do on stage. Ballet or
modern or whatever. Chor-e-o-graphed. Someone tells
the dancers who went to special schools for years and
years where to move and what to feel and they do that. A
bunch of people—the ODD-ience—watches. They love it
or hate it or don't give a shit. They clap...they applaud.

No matter what they feel the people watching, they
always applaud.
Two. Ballroom dancing. Like waltzing. Two people
dance together, touching and that in a certain way. In
ballroom dancing they say you don't need an oddience but
far as I can see you do. This oddience though they almost
never applaud. Except in movies.
Three. Social dancing. This happens at parties
sometimes, at wedding receptions and clubs and bars. In
this kind there's also couples and it's social because it's
not planned out or anything. For fun. Mostly for fun, and
for mating purposes. You know, sex.
There's about thirteen, fifteen ways to do this kind of
dancing but there's also all this subtle stuff that changes
with each person. One time people did certain styles of
social dancing. The Mashed Potato. The Cha Cha Cha.
The Pony The Hustle The Stroll. Then all these got
together with Ballroom Dancing and turned into
Disc-O-Dancing but that does not exist on this planet
anymore.
In Social Dancing the movements of the dancers is
usually pretty uptight because of an unhappy childhood or
a very heavy neurosis about death or whatever.
Sometimes the movements are free and that but this only
happens when the brain gets taken over by some chemical
like booze or drugs.
And people watch. But no way, no way do they applaud.

Then there is the best kind of dancing.
Four. This kind doesn't have a name. I could make one
up. But I won't. This kind there's no oddience, no steps,
no anything, just you. It can happen anytime, anywhere.
And the most beautiful...the best ever music is playing.
And it's REEEEEALY LOUD! But it doesn't hurt your
ears. But just really like there are about a hundred million
speakers all around you and each one plays only one note,
but perfectly. And everything is...everything.
And the whole world is alive, every tree, every chair,

every everything. And you feel everything, and you can
hear everybody really clapping. And yes. Yes yes yes yes
yes....And I am one with the music, I am the music and
the dancing and all is one and everything and nothing and
I am floating flying flying dancing dancing dancing...

> STEVE *raises his arm in the air which*
> *pulls the chain tight around his neck*
> *making him gag.*

It is very important as one matures to draw a thick dark
line between dreams and reality. Four.

> IMAGE: *"Four".* SOUND: *applause.*
> *Black. Lights up on* STEVE *facing a white*
> *birdcage hanging in the space. In the cage*
> *is a large white egg.*

(*to egg*) There's only one of me. It's just you and me.
And you are mine.
(*to audience*) Somebody gives you something.
Somebody in your family or somebody you are "with" or
somebody you just met or somebody you don't even like
but they give you something and even if you don't want it
it's yours.
(*to egg*) Because there's only one of me and they gave
you to me so you're mine.
(*to audience*) And I, me, I, can do anything anything
anything I want with what's mine. Right?

> *Pause.*

(*to egg*) See!
(*to audience*) So, all you got to figure out is what to do
with it.

> *Pause.*

After you figure out: what it is.

> *Black.* MUSIC: *"Jesus, Lifeline of My
> Soul"* . *Lights up on* STEVE *standing on
> the chair with a noose around his neck.*

Don't freak out eh. Everybody needs an option.

> SCREEN IMAGE: *"Op-tion"*.

OP-TION.
That's a good idea eh? You either do this or you do that.
You either have toast or you have cereal. You either get
out of bed in the morning or you throw the clock across
the room. This is my option. And this here (*stamps chair*)
is my step to my option. See?
So.
I can either wait around here for something really truly
real to happen or…I can climb my stairway to heaven.

I'm full of beauty eh. Metaphors and that. Full of it. Man,
I'm so full of beauty I could just…die.

> STEVE *laughs until he snorts. He snorts
> until he cries. Black.* SCREEN IMAGE: *A
> window. Lights up.* STEVE *faces the
> scrim, his back to the audience. He makes
> his hands move as the voice of the egg and
> the sperm making shadow puppets on the
> scrim.*

The sperm and the egg. The sperm. And. The egg.
The sperm and the egg.
"Stevie."
The sperm and the egg.
"Stevie!"
The sperm—
"STEVIE!"

What!
"Here's your rosary."
I don't need it.
"You take your beads!
Have you got your ticket Stevie?"
Yeah.
"And here I made you up some bologna sandwiches for
the plane. And don't you go hungry for pride! And here,
your long underwear."
Ma!
"Stevie, just because you're leaving home doesn't mean
you're not going to get cold anymore. And take these."
What are they?
"Just take them. Put one in each pocket."

What for?
"STEVIE JUST DO AS I SAY!"

     STEVE *turns and addresses the audience.*

Little pieces of paper and on each one she had all filled
out: my name, my address, my phone number and I AM A
CATHOLIC PLEASE CALL A PRIEST.

     STEVE *turns back.*

Ma I told you a hundred times, I'm not a Catholic
anymore.
"STEVIE! You were born a Catholic of two Catholics
you were christened a Catholic confirmed a Catholic you
went to Catholic school and you will be a Catholic for all
eternity whether you like it or not!"

     Pause.

Why one in every pocket?
"Because. In case the plane was to crash and you were to

get all burned up or split apart there'd be a better chance
they'd find one."

The egg. And. Theeeeeee Sperm! (*bringing up the other
hand*)

Bye Da.
"Stevie?"
What?
"Uh. You uh. You. Watch yourself."
Okay.
"Stevie..."
Yeah?
"You...Listen to me now."
What?
"Just. Don't go getting in any trouble."
I won't.
"But just..."
What!
"You just keep your pecker in your pants until you find a
girl you want to marry!"

> *The* IMAGE *of the window disappears.*
> STEVE *steps into shaft of light.*

Doesn't every kid want to have a black room? An
all-black room? I did. All black. The walls black, the
ceiling black, the floor black and black curtains on the
window so only one little stream of light comes through
and in it you see all the dust and shit in the air. Yeah!
They wouldn't let me though. Most kids don't get their
black room they got to spend their whole life looking for
it.
The sperm and the egg.
The sperm and the egg.
The sperm and the egg.
The sperm and the egg!

If my sperm had ever hit an egg, I would've let the kid
have it's black room right away and got it over with.

> *Black.* SOUND: *whistling. Lights up.*
> STEVE *is whistling into the cage.*

I had a cat once. It didn't have a name. People think that's
weird eh. Not naming a cat. But you know what? I don't
think they want names. And when me and the cat were
alone in the house? I'd do this...I'd do this certain series
of...acts to it.
Interest peaked?

First. I'd throw him across the bedroom ten or twelve
times. Not into a wall or anything, just onto the bed.
Second, I'd grab his front paws in one hand, his back
paws in the other hand and swing him around for thirteen
fifteen seconds. Then, I'd take the lid off the garbage can,
put him in the garbage can, put the lid on the garbage can
and bang on the sides: bangbangbangbangbangbangbang
bangbangbang real fast for, I don't know, ten seconds.
Then! Oh man!

Then I'd take the lid off the can and STAND BACK!
That cat would fly!
FLY! I can't describe it, it's just something you've got to
see.
FLY! And then disappear for like an hour, maybe more.
But. I didn't LIKE doing that to him. I didn't do that to
him because I liked it. It was to see him fly. And! And the
real reason why I did it was to help him realize how lucky
he was to have it's freedom.

> *Pause.*

But you know what? You could tell that, like after awhile,
after he got over it and that, like a day or something later,
you could tell by the way he stretched into the sunlight on

the livingroom carpet, you could tell, he didn't remember a goddamn thing about it. Fucking cats eh?

> *Pause.*

I'm glad I told you that.

> *Black.* SCREEN IMAGE: *"possi." Lights up.* STEVE *is opening the cage.* SCREEN IMAGE: *"bili." Throughout the following* STEVE *takes the egg from the cage and holds it up to the light.*

It might be. It might be. It might be. It might be. It might be. It might be. It might be.

> STEVE *replaces the egg and closes the cage door.*

It might be.

> *Lights fade.* SCREEN IMAGE: *"ties."* MUSIC: *loud rock.* STEVE *is straddling the chair, laughing.*

This buddy of mine? This old buddy of mine. Crab. Crab, that was his name. Good guy excellent guy. Haven't seen him in...Big tall guy. And he had these hands right? Both his hands. Each one had a thumb, like a normal thumb, but his four fingers, these four fingers on both hands were all mushed up together, all joined together like one great big finger. Shit he was a funny guy. And we'd go out right, like to meet people at some bar or something and say like there'd be these people he never met before? He'd come in, sit down, be like: "Hi" "Hello" and he'd say: "I'm Crab" right? And they'd be like: yeah right whatever; then, after a couple of minutes, he'd take his hands and put them up flat on the table like

this. Right okay? Like this. Then, all of a sudden, like
one by one maybe, everybody'd notice. And it would get
reeeeealy quiet. Quiet but like loud so you're deaf from
it. Nobody could talk and I'm trying not to break up
cause I know what's coming. Then, sure as shit man sure
as shit, some dick'd go: "Um, what did you say your
name was?"
And he'd go: (*waving his hands in the air like claws*)
"Crab."! Oh man it was beautiful. Crab? Get it get it!
Oh man. They'd freak out. Shit.
And you know what?
Nobody'd mention his hands. NOBODY'D MENTION
HIS FUCKING HANDS!
And you know what else? Crab didn't give a sweet shit.
ALL RIGHT BUDDY! Man, Crab could handle anything.
Made me wish I was born without a nose or something.

> STEVE *covers his nose with one hand*
> *and extends the other.*

Hi there.
Beak.

> *Black.* STEVE *sits up centre in the chair.*

Shit.

> SCREEN IMAGE: *"shit."*

Shit man shit. Shit shit shit.
Everything is shit. Everywhere is shit. Everywhere you
read, you turn on the TV, the radio: Shit! Buy this do that
be this.
Shit!
People. People you talk to.
People sticking their holes right up against your ear and
taking a big long shit into your brain. Then you come
home what do you have to do? You have to shit!

Shit!
But that doesn't do nothing. You can shit your head off
but you're still full of it.
Every teeny tiny little cell man. And you can poke and
pull and squeeeeeeeeeze...But man, there's no way you
can get it all out. No way. Still there. Oh! But...Shit's
good right? Yeah. It's good.
Cause: everybody's got it and everybody does it and it's
what keeps us all humble and makes us all the same.
So, that's what it is.

> *Pause.*

WELL THAT'S FUCKING ENCOURAGING!

> *Black.* SOUND: *a crowded bar, fades*
> *throughout next scene. Lights up.* STEVE
> *is standing with a chair.*

Okay, you're out in some bar or something and you're
talking to someone or yourself...or someone say, and
you're just talking and that and doing what you do when
you talk that you don't even know that you do but you do
that you don't even think about but you do. Making
faces. Weird faces.
Sitting funny with your head stuck out say.
And you've got your arms like this say and you're going
like this. You're telling a story about how you came this
close to winning something. Money say.
Or how you got fired for telling your boss to take this job
and shove it and his whole goddamn family especially his
ugly daughter...And you notice this jerk...Over on the
other side of the bar. You can just see him out of the
corner of your eye but you can tell the guy's a jerk. So
you just think: "Jerk" and keep going.
Then it's getting weird: This jerk is sort of looking at you
it looks like.
"What's that jerk looking at?" So... You stop telling your

story. And you're all ready to look at this jerk and make
this face of: "What's your problem?" or whatever.

> STEVE *turns to face jerk.*

It's a mirror.

> *Black. Lights up.* STEVE *is sitting*
> *diagonally across from the cage.*

Hey!
Hey hey hey hey!
Hey! You!
Come here.
You! Hey! Come here!
What are you waiting for?
What are you waiting for?

> STEVE *approaches the egg.*

What are you waiting for, I am asking you what you are
waiting for! Don't you know it's RUDE not to answer a
person's question? Didn't you mother ever teach you—

> *Pause.*

Yeah yeah sorry sorry.

> STEVE *sits on floor facing egg.*

You don't smoke do you?

> *Black.* SOUND: *a rattlesnake.* STEVE
> *approaches the cage singing.*

"L is for the way you Look at me. O is for the only One I
see. V is Very very extraordinary. E is Even more
than…"

SCREEN IMAGE: *a heart.*

Funny about that eh?
You make this friend. You make this friend at a party or
the laund-ro-mat. You make this friend. You like this
person. You spend time with this person. A lot of time.
You tell this person here things about yourself, your
family. Secret things. Things you always thought were
secrets. This person sees you naked. In the daytime. You
put your mouth on this person. On their body. Places you
never thought you'd touch with your mouth. But you do.
And you like it. Because. This person is your friend.
Because you...
Oh yeah.
Oh yeah oh yeah oh baby oh yeah yes yeah yes do that
yes do that yes oh yeah oh baby oh baby oh baby...

A scream begins. No sound.

There it is!
People scream eh?
They're supposed to.
Even if you're by yourself you should scream
because...it's scary! Never worry about screaming.
Shake the walls, crack the ceiling, let the curtain in the
temple be rent in two...oh yeah. What you got to worry
about is if there's no scream. Man if somebody doesn't
scream then you better get help. Because everybody
should scream when they come.
You know why they call it come?
They call it come because you come...this close...to
nothing. That's what it is, where everything is nothing
and you are not and the whole world is like this big huge
lung so full it's about to explode but this big huge lung
full of...nothing. Zero. That close to zero. They call it
the big "0" but it's not though, not "OH," it's ZERO.
Being zero. Nothing. No things. No thoughts. No
feelings. Only...

Doesn't it just make you want to scream though?
Oh yeah.
Oh yeah oh yeah oh baby oh yeah yes yeah yes do that
yes do that yes oh yeah oh baby oh baby oh baby...I
LOVE YOU!!!
Ooops.

Looooovvvvvve. It doesn't exist really. That kind of
L-O-V-E, Nat King Cole kind of love does not.
Well it does. For virgins...and pop singers...and poets.
That love is actually just fear wearing nice perfume.
That's what someone once told me. Fear.
"The terror of knowing that you have put yourself in a
position where another human being has control over you
and might, and probably will, do everything they can to
destroy you." TO DESTROY YOU!
Love is fear in a nice neighborhood.
And there's alot of energy out there calling itself love and
you never know when you might turn a corner and
BLAM! find yourself inside it.
So you have to be careful.
I'm not bitter or anything.
Love does not exist.
Love is lust. Fear. Yeah.

Pause.

(*to audience*) BOO!

STEVE *laughs. Pause.*

(*to egg*) Boo.

SCREEN IMAGE: *"boo." Black. Lights
up.* STEVE *is in the chair leaning
against the SL wall.*

I go to this diner.

Not a rest-o-rant I hate rest-o-rants I never go to
rest-o-rants I only go to diners. And I only go to diners
that have all day breakfasts because who the hell are they
to tell me when I should eat breakfast? Who the hell are
they to tell me when I should get out of bed? This
particular breakfast this particular day was three, four
o'clock. Sausages, hash browns, WHITE toast, BLACK
coffee and eggs over EASY! Very easy, so you can still
taste the rawness in the yolk; so you can
almost…taste…that…chicken.

Sometimes jam sometimes not depends on the day this
day no. So I'm sitting there looking out the window
thinking about how when trees are dead and the leaves are
gone you can see so much more of the world and this
woman four, four and a half feet away left side starts
talking to her friend in this pretty loud voice about this
trip she took to Mexico.

"There were so many Gringos."

Yeah. I'm serious. Gringos. That's what she said.

And then? Everytime the guy brings something over to
the table she goes "Gracias!"

Gracias like she took one trip there and she turns into
fucking Mexico. But that be okay, but that be okay until
she starts talking about being on this bus with all these
"Men" and she says "Men" like it's some kind of disease
or a new drug. "Men."

And what am I? I'm a man. I'm a man sitting right there.
She'd be looking right at me if she'd just turn her head
this much. She practically is staring at me without even
moving her eyes at all. I'm right there!

Then! Out of nowhere, she's telling her friend about the
Grand Canyon. The fucking Grand Canyon's not in
Mexico!

What am I supposed to think right?

THEN! Fuck…Then she's describing this dream she had
where all these "Men" are growing out of the walls in her
apartment. All these "Men." So I was pretty fed up

right—
And not because she's a woman, don't think that okay, I
got nothing against women—
Fake mothers I do! Fake mothers who come up to you in
rest-o-rants and stab you in the guts with a fork I do! But
this woman here it was just her Person-Ality that was
pissing me off...and how she was saying all this shit just
so somebody would hear her. I'm sitting right there!
So.
So I lean over and I say: "Excuse me. Why don't you go
get some help!" Yeah I did.
No I didn't.
l didn't say that. What I said was: "If you want to sleep
with me why don't you just say so?"
No I didn't.
l didn't say nothing.
Crab would've though. First though he would've waved
his hands around a bit.

>   *Pause.*

But you know what I did do though?
l got up, and I changed my seat!
That's almost as good as saying something.
And I never went back to that diner either.
Not because of her...but because they got my fucking
eggs wrong!

>   *Black.* SOUND: *a cuckoo clock strikes*
>   *three.* SCREEN IMAGE: *"False Mother*
>   *#2."* Lights up. STEVE *is centrestage.*

Beware the cuckoo!
Oh yeah, everybody thinks they're so great. Those
wooden clocks and that. HA! I can just see those little
cuckoo bastards rubbing their little wings together and
laughing over that one.
The female cuckoo, when she's going to have a baby

finds another kind of bird's nest with new laid eggs in it
and lays her egg there. Her ONE egg. And then she just
takes off to fuck knows where. The other bird comes
home and figures she just counted wrong or something
and starts hatching it with the other eggs...So
anyway...the cuckoo egg hatches first, the mother bird
just thinks it's a preemie or something and goes out
looking for food for it. And then, fuck, this little cuckoo
bastard pushes all the other eggs out of the nest, the real
children, so it can have all the food for itself. The fake
mother bird? She goes for it. Just a run of bad luck she
thinks.
Now.
You might think that this fake mother bird is stupid or
something for letting herself be duped like that but NO!
See it's trust. Blind trust man. This is her kid we're
talking about here, she thinks it's her kid. She fucking
loves this egg. Fuck.
So anyway, this fake mother bird feeds this jerk-off
cuckoo. Feeds it and feeds it and feeds it until it's big
enough to fly away...and then it just fucking takes
off...nothing, not a howd'ya do, nothing. Gone.
It's wild. Fucking abandonment man. Abandonment.
Big stuff. Really big stuff. Like you know? Big time.
Fuck man, the cuckoo's got no heart.
The cuckoo's got no fucking heart!

Black. Lights up. STEVE *is squatting
centrestage.*

I am a unique person.
I am special.
I am a unique and special one of a kind person.
I am not like anyone else.
I am myself and that is like nothing else in this or any
other world.

Pause.

This is earth right? We're on earth. And we know these planets: Mercury, Venus, Earth, Mars, Jupiter, Saturn, Uranus, Neptune. Pluto. And they all move around the sun. At the middle. But all these planets go around the sun and at the same time they're spinning around themselves in tiny little circles. Going around and spinning at the same time. AND each, or most, of these planets have moons. Little planets that go around these other first planets. Earth's just got one moon but some planets have more, one planet's got like SEVEN or something! So. Going around and spinning and going around all this frigging moving okay? And we're on Earth. And we're all moving around stuff all the time, even when we sleep. And there are, I don't know, billions of people on Earth, zillions, trillions, whatever that is but it's like more than anybody could every count in like a hundred lifetimes or whatever.

BUT!

I am a unique person. I am special. I am a unique and special one of a kind person. I am not like anyone else. I am myself and that is like nothing else in this or any other world.
FUCK!

Pause.

Fuuuuuuuck.

Black. Lights up. STEVE is bouncing off the walls in the space.

Like...like...like...like like like. Walking around walking around walking around or in a room full of people a box full of people arms legs eyes feet faces stuff and BRAINS! BRAINS! BRAINS! In every person is a

brain! ALL these brains in shells all over the place.
Think now.

       Pause.

See!
That was your brain working that was your BRAIN!
That's where all the action is. Inside's where. So how
come I can't see the action? How come! (*noticing egg*)
Maybe...Maybe it might be that. Okay.
Say. Say. Say this here egg here. All you see is the shell,
but that's nothing, all the real stuff, all the live stuff, that's
inside.
I could...break it open. I could. Then I'd see it.
But then it'd be dead.
I could...cook it and eat it.
But then it be shit.
No.
Just like this here.
This is how it's an egg.
You just gotta wait.
All right then.
I'll wait.

       Pause.

Man oh man I would really really really like to have a
little chat with God.

       Black. SOUND: *rattling of a chain. Lights*
       up on STEVE *counting the links of a*
       chain.

The chain man. Chain. The chain. See, the whole
frigging world is all wrapped up in this great big chain.
The whole frigging world. And this chain, it's made up of
these things. These things: You're born. You work. You
die. You're born you work you die you're born you work

you die you're born you work you die you're born you
work and like that. And inside that there's all this other
stuff. Stuff. You eat you sleep you shit you breathe you
eat you sleep you shit you breathe you eat you sleep you
shit you. Okay? But it's all this big chain around
everything. Now. You take one of those things, say you
take "you breathe," you take "you breathe" and you say "I
am not going to do that anymore." So you don't. You
stop breathing. You hold your breath.

Pause.

Then, either you change your mind and start breathing
again or...you kick off. And even if you do kick off
you're lucky if maybe two maybe ONE person is even
fucked up about it for like a year right? And that's lucky.
Because? Life goes on, right? Right? Life goes on. It
doesn't go over or up or down or whatever. It doesn't go
BUUUUUUUZZZZZZZZ, it doesn't go
VAAAAAAAAAAARRRRRRRROOOOOOOOOMMM
MMM, or like that. It goes...ON. Life goes on.

STEVE *approaches cage and spins it*
violently.

On and on and on and on and on and on and on and on
and on and on and on and on. Because everybody's
everybody's everybody's...!
Alright.
Alright.
I'm coming home.

STEVE *places chair downstage centre.*

I'm coming home.
I'm coming home and I'm walking up the sidewalk I'm
walking up the sidewalk and there's my house and I see
my house and I get to my house and I turn to walk up the

steps—
And there's this guy on the lawn. Laying on the lawn.
The front lawn of where I live. I think: Oh so he's passed
out, but no, his eyes are open. So, he's having a little rest.
I go on my way. Then I hear him, breathing. He's really
stiff right and he's breathing like this. Through his teeth.
Like he's running really fast. But he's not. He's really
still right. And I think: Maybe I should go over and ask
this guy is he okay and then I think what a stupid fucking
question that would be cause look at the guy he's not
okay. So I'm just gonna go in. Then he's talking. But not
to me. He's looking up at the sky and talking through his
teeth saying: COME ON COME ON COME ON COME
ON COME ON COME ON COME ON.
I stop for a second. Then I go in the house.
And I go upstairs and I stand in the front window and I
watch this guy.
I can't hear him but I can see he's still breathing through
his teeth and going: COME ON COME ON COME ON
COME ON COME ON.
I watch this guy, all day, and I ask myself…
What. Is. He. Waiting. For.
What?
WHAT THE FUCK IS HE WAITING FOR? What am I
waiting for? What's everybody waiting for? Everybody's
waiting. Everybody's waiting for something.
(*to egg*) You hear me? You hear me? What am I waiting
for? What? For some life to start? For some woman who
I think is my mother to come up and stab me in the guts
with a fork? For some life to end? What!
Well I'm sick! You hear me? I'm sick. I'm sick of waiting.
And I'm through waiting for YOU!

> STEVE *strikes the birdcage with the*
> *chair. Black.* SOUND: *crushing metal,*
> *shattering glass, a flock of birds, a high C,*
> *a siren. Lights up.* STEVE *is sitting on the*
> *chair, centrestage. He is panting.*

The day Alphonse McKeigan killed the duck in
Wentworth Park I was there. Alphonse and the boys were
over across the pond and I was sitting on this side
watching them. I had a book. I was pretending to read a
book. I used to do that when I was a kid, pretend to be
reading a book so I could watch things. They were
smoking cigarettes and laughing. Then they go around to
behind the bandshell where the pond gets smaller. After a
few minutes I hear all this yelling and splashing and that
and I figure Alphonse threw in his brother Victor or some
other of those assholes so I go around to see. I get there
they're all throwing rocks into the middle. I don't know
what they're throwing at. I don't see nothing.
Then I see it.
This duck.
They're just missing it.
And then this duck, it swims right for me. Right at me.
I'm almost getting hit by these rocks now and this duck it
comes right up by me. Trying to get up the bank, and it
does, the boys come tearing across the pond after it like
they were walking on water. Chasing this duck. And they
get it, caught up by the fence. The boys fall back and it's
just Alphonse and the duck. He's going at it with these
rocks, I don't know where they're coming from. WAP
WAP, picking up rocks that already hit it and giving it to
him again, WAP WAP. And I'm thinking: I should do
something or even just yell or something. But I don't,
first I think it's cause I'm scared but it's not. It's cause I
want to watch. This guy is killing something. Killing
something!
I never seen anything get killed before. That must
be...that must be the most power in the whole world. The
most power in the whole world.

> *The noose is flown in.* STEVE *fixates on
> it.* SOUND: *elongated birdcage smash,
> siren etc.*

There's only one of me. There's only one of me. There's only one of me. There's only one of me. ONE. There's only one of me there's only one of me there's only one of me there's only one of me. TWO. There's only one of me there's only one of me there's only one of me there's only one of me there's only one of me. THREE.

Silence.

There's only one of me.
There is only one of me.
Four.

STEVE *knocks the chair over.*

Dance dance dance dance dance dance dance dance!

Black.

The End.